College TO Career
JOURNAL

101 Thought-Provoking Ways to Help
You Land the Job of Your Dreams

JOHN P. DOYLE

INDIE BOOKS
INTERNATIONAL

ISBN: 1941870023
ISBN 13: 9781941870020
Library of Congress Control Number: 2014952545

Designed by Joni McPherson, mcphersongraphics.com

INDIE BOOKS INTERNATIONAL, LLC
2424 VISTA WAY, SUITE 316
OCEANSIDE, CA 92054
www.indiebooksintl.com

➤ Contents ◀

Resume Preparation

Cover Letter Preparation

Interview Preparation

Behavioral Interview Techniques

Potential Interview Questions

Candidate Questions

Networking

➤ Dedication ◄

There are thousands of college graduates entering the job market every year. The world we live in is fast-paced, competitive, and social media rich. Information is one click away from us all to retrieve answers that would have taken hours or days in years past. All of the latest technology has impacted how we see the world today.

Grads are in Generation Y or commonly referred to as millenials, having grown up in this age of technology. They are attached to tablets, smart phones, computer games and the like, which puts these young men and women in a precarious position. The inability to effectively communicate face-to-face and handle social situations has been a growing concern.

I dedicate this book to all the young men and women needing direction in building their brand to land the job of their dreams. And to my children, Johnny and Natalya, who are about to start their college journey, my hope is I made an impact in your life to appreciate my love, guidance, and support. Your education is a gift and never to be taken for granted.

John P. Doyle

➤ Acknowledgements ◄

My father, John J. Doyle, was a young man when he passed away in 1967. He left behind Mom, my sister Donna, my brother Mike, and me. We were very young when he was taken from us. Dad was a family man with a kind soul and a zest for life. Many that knew him say I have his character and personality. I thank him for everything he taught me. He has been watching from above, guiding me to know right from wrong. I am sure he is proud of what I have accomplished, and more importantly, proud of my mother, Dorothy Doyle O'Connor who was left to raise our young family. Mom taught me to be strong, never to give up and get through rough times. I remember her telling me repeatedly, "You are John Doyle, and you can do anything when you put your mind to it." This has resonated with me throughout my life. Mom taught me to be confident and secure with myself. I am forever thankful for everything she did, making the best of a life-changing situation.

Aunt Marlene and Uncle Mike, thank you for being there for our family, helping Mom raise my sister, my brother and me. Uncle Mike, rest in peace. You were always there for me in the absence of Dad.

To my lovely wife, Natalie, you have been my best friend and supporter and always encouraged me to share my knowledge. You are strong-willed, intelligent and comforting. Colonel, you are my soul mate and I love you dearly.

To my children, Johnny and Natalya, my life became complete when you came to this country as young children. You are the future and represent what my book represents. Your future is extremely bright, and I love the both of you more than you know.

To Russ Riendeau from East Wing Search Group, who suggested I write a book, thank you for the advice.

To Henry DeVries, my publisher and editor, thank you for taking my project and making my dream a reality. Your encouragement and ideas are appreciated.

To all my former colleagues I have enjoyed working for and with over the years:

Jim Critchfield, thank you for taking a chance hiring me as a young kid in 1982. You taught me how to be a great sales executive and manager, and we had fun all the while.

Martin Rogman, thank you for holding me accountable and pushing my skills to the limit. It certainly was a life lesson under your leadership.

Jim Butts, Brad Clark, Nikki DeYoung, Tom Kotopka, Eric Butt, Tim Joyce, Pete Lombardo, Bill Austin, and many other managers over the years, our time together was special. The fun stories and memories will last a lifetime.

Finally, to other colleagues that made my job easier, thank you. Dave Niemeyer, Nick Gillespie, Helen Sweet, Brian Puzey, Tim Cook, Keith Davison, Todd Ferguson, Denise Senior, Mary Campbell, and too many others to mention, your success was my success and I am grateful for our time together.

⟫ Introduction – How to Use This Book ⟨

Congratulations, you've completed your college journey. Now what do you do? How do you turn your degree into a career? This guide has the information you need to get started on the journey from college to career.

Securing a job is a job in itself, and one that many of us are not prepared properly for upon leaving our college or university. Job hunting and interviewing are specialized skills that can be likened to muscles that need to be developed and toned over time. This journal is designed to help you build your career-searching muscles through a series of exercises and thought provoking questions. It is designed as an open book test, providing you the necessary skills and confidence to feel more comfortable and certain of your career ahead.

What you'll get from this guide:
- What to include in your resume and cover letter
- How to prepare for an interview
- How to answer behavioral interview questions
- Over forty sample interview questions
- How to build your network

You can begin to use the journal anytime during your college career, but no later than the start of your junior year. Your answers can be written on each page. Upon completion, you will be amazed when you see all the answers to the test. Your career search will become smoother, building your confidence and making you feel more comfortable and certain of what lies ahead. Put some time into each section and think about your answers. The more preparation you put in now will increase your brand and more importantly, earning potential.

We wish you the best of luck in your career search.

Your journey begins now!

1

Resume Preparation

Resumes are the roadmap of the past eight years of your life and need to be written to tell your life story. Unfortunately, your recent relative work experiences cannot tell the interviewer your story regarding the successes and impact you will make in their company. However, involvement in clubs, organizations, sports, and philanthropic causes are a solid indication to the hiring manager of the type of person you are. Companies hiring entry-level positions look for all of these activities that define your character and brand. Therefore, it is critical when preparing your resume to emphasize all your accomplishments in these areas.

_____

_____

_____

_____

_____

_____

_____

_____

_____

_____

_____

_____

_____

_____

_____

_____

2

Career Objective

Your career aspiration defines your goals and objectives. It is the defining declaration of how you will be branding your talent to a prospective employer. So, what talent and value can you bring to the hiring manager? Is your talent unique? Will it catch the eye of the search engine or hiring manager reviewing your resume? Be specific, including your experiences that are relative to the position. Provide timelines and dates that you would like to see your objectives accomplished.

In the space below, make notes on possible career objectives.

3

Work History: High School

Note: Think back as far as you can—when did you begin to earn money? Were you cutting lawns, babysitting, shoveling snow, washing cars? These are all the jobs you want to be able to speak to during the interview which demonstrate responsibility at a young age. *They will not be listed on your resume.*

_____

_____

_____

_____

_____

High School: Now it's time to list positions you held when you officially became of legal age to work. High school jobs are taken to earn money for college or maybe a used car, but more importantly, to learn responsibility. Was that you? However, if you were employed in a position matching your career interests, employers will like that, because it demonstrates responsibility and maturity at a young age. Such positions would include, but are not limited to, sales, technical work in IT, accounting, tutoring young children, etc.

_____

_____

_____

_____

_____

4

Work History: College

What type of positions did you hold in college? Were they relative to your career aspirations? If so, this will be the time to tie these experiences and the impact you can make from those experiences to the organization. How many hours per week did you work? Did you hold more than one job? Were you able to participate in other extra-curricular activities? Did work get in the way? What was your GPA? Were you able to maintain or increase your GPA while you were working?

_____

_____

_____

_____

_____

_____

_____

_____

_____

_____

_____

_____

_____

_____

_____

_____

_____

5

Work History: College Summer Employment

Were you able to keep your position from high school or did you find other employment during the three summers you were not attending school? Did you complete an internship? If so, was it relative to your area of interest? Employers like students that participated in summer internships. They can begin as early as upon completion of freshman year.

_____

_____

_____

_____

_____

_____

_____

_____

_____

_____

_____

_____

_____

_____

_____

_____

_____

_____

6

Leadership: High School

Were you involved in high school government? Did you hold any leadership position in extra-curricular activities? Did you hold any supervisory roles as a young teen while working? Were you the captain of your sport? Did you volunteer for philanthropic causes and hold any leadership positions?

_____

_____

_____

_____

_____

_____

_____

_____

_____

_____

_____

_____

_____

_____

_____

_____

_____

7

Leadership: College

Were you involved in college government? Did you hold any leadership position in extra-curricular activities? Did you hold any supervisory roles as a young teen while working? Were you the captain of your sport? Did you volunteer for philanthropic causes and hold any leadership positions?

Same as high school, right? Here are a few more to consider. Were you in a fraternity or sorority? If so, did you hold any offices? Were you involved in professional associations or clubs? If so, did you hold a leadership role? Were you the one that was elected to be the team leader for school class projects?

_____

_____

_____

_____

_____

_____

_____

_____

_____

_____

_____

_____

_____

_____

_____

8

Resume Writing

Now that you've brainstormed the information to include, let's talk about how to construct the resume. Review all of your subheadings and make sure they align in terms of structure, capitalization, and font size. Use bullet points in short sentences to structure the body of the resume. The main selling points should be clear and easy to scan quickly. Don't worry about the specifics; you will be able to expand on these during the meeting. Keep your resume to one page. It may be hard, but focus on things that are important to land the position. List your GPA. Be specific.

9

Relevant Classes

Did you take classes that are relevant to the position you are interviewing? If so, list them; for instance, operations management, sales management, and international economics. Be specific and list what you can offer that another candidate can't. Do not embellish the truth. Be prepared to back up your class accomplishments. Bring in class projects. You never can be too prepared.

10

Your Strengths

Your strengths are the key to the hiring manager. Having an impactful and truthful career objective is crucial to get noticed. The average time a hiring manager reviews an incoming resume is no more than 30 seconds. Post your best strengths first that will support the position. You are baiting hiring managers with your brand and you need to reel them in.

11

$ and %

Hiring managers like to see $ and % signs in a resume. Have you had a job in high school or college that had responsibility and accountability for an increase in sales and customer satisfaction? How about reduction in costs or reduced turnover? Were you able to tutor that young child to ace the exam?

Leadership roles in fraternity, sorority, clubs, or volunteer work will have an impact. The leader is always asked to make a contribution to increase or decrease something. Is that you?

12

Accentuate the Positive

Focus on the positive career events in your life. No need to bring up the negative. Hiring managers are looking for positive colleagues that will have an impact to their business. Any positive events you could bring up that you haven't already covered?

_____

_____

_____

_____

_____

_____

_____

_____

_____

_____

_____

_____

_____

_____

_____

_____

_____

_____

13

Keywords

Does the position you are interviewing for match your bulleted strengths and keywords on your resume? How do you find out? Look at the job posting or other similar postings and match your skill sets to the position. Do yourself a big favor: do not apply for positions that do not match your skill sets. You will be wasting your time and the hiring manager's time as well.

Write down some keywords that come to mind.

_____

_____

_____

_____

_____

_____

_____

_____

_____

_____

_____

_____

_____

_____

_____

_____

14

Action Words A - E

Many companies today are using sophisticated software to electronically scan resumes, looking for action words relative to the position. The software is looking for words that have been chosen by the hiring manager. Review other job postings relative to your aspirations and look for common words and add them to your resume. Some of these words are as follows—commonly applicable words are in bold.

Circle the words that fit you best.

A: achieved, accomplished, assisted, analyzed

B: budgeted, built

C: compiled, **created**, coordinated, communicated, contributed, calculated, collaborated, contracted, conducted, counseled, consolidated, contributed, completed, capitalized

D: developed, demonstrated, directed, doubled, designed, determined, **decreased**

E: exercised, engineered, engaged, endorsed, expedited, elected, entered, eliminated

15

Action Words F - K

Circle the words that fit you best.

F: facilitated, focused, financed, figured

G: garnered, granted, generated, guided

H: handled, helped, hired, hosted

I: improved, **increased**, identified, implemented, inaugurated, installed, inspired, issued, incurred, innovated, informed, illustrated, instructed , inspired, influenced, ideas, invented

J: judged, joined

16

Action Words L - Q

Circle the words that fit you best.

L: launched, litigated, lobbied, located, leadership, led

M: managed, maintained, measured, mastered, motivated, modified, minimized, marketed, mapped, maximized, modeled, monitored

N: negotiated, noticed, nurtured, narrated

O: optimized, opened, operated, oversaw, overhauled, organized, observed, obtained, oriented, orchestrated, originated

P: participated, **profits**, prevented, proposed, preserved, processed, pioneered, prioritized, planned, prepared, presented, provided, persuaded, probed, programmed, projected, promoted, published, placed

Q: quantified, quoted

17

Action Words: R - Z

Circle the words that fit you best.

R: resolved, revenue, ranked, raised, redesigned, recruited, resonated, reduced, replaced, resolved, represented, reconciled, recommended, recorded, researched, remodeled, renegotiated, reorganized, restructured, repaired, retained, retrieved, revamped, rewarded

S: secured, stabilized, saved, scheduled, screened, simplified, spearheaded, substantiated, streamlined, strategized, stimulated, supported, structured, substituted, settled, steered, supplied, specified, staffed, staged, standardized, suggested, surpassed, selected, strengthened, stressed

T: tabulated, transferred, **trained,** transformed, tailored, targeted, taught, testified, transported, tailored, terminated, tested, traveled

U: utilized, uncovered, unified, undertook, updated, upgraded

V: volunteered, validated, verified, valued, viewed

W: won, weighed, welcomed, widened, witnessed, worked, wrote

18

References

References are presented on a separate document. It is recommended to have a minimum of three. Include former professors, former or existing employers, college or high school coaches, fraternity or sorority executives, and professional association or club executives. Do not include personal friends or immediate family members.

Make a list of potential references.

_____

_____

_____

_____

_____

_____

_____

_____

_____

_____

_____

_____

_____

_____

_____

_____

_____

19

Letters of Recommendation

Ask your references for a letter of recommendation that can be attached to your reference document. They will be happy to help.

Make a list of who you will contact and note your deadline.

_____

_____

_____

_____

_____

_____

_____

_____

_____

_____

_____

_____

_____

_____

_____

_____

_____

_____

_____

_____

20

References Document

Reference documentation should be presented on the same heavy stock paper as your resume.

References should be presented as follows:

Name of person, job title, and employment

Affiliation the person has to you (professor, former employer, etc.)

Phone number

E-mail address

21

Give References a Heads Up

One last thing: make sure to call your references, informing them that someone from your potential employer will be calling. It's nice to give them a heads up so they can be better prepared for the conversation. Are there references you need to call?

_____

_____

_____

_____

_____

_____

_____

_____

_____

_____

_____

_____

_____

_____

_____

_____

_____

_____

_____

_____

22

Cover Letter Preparation

Ah, the dreaded cover letter. Many college grads are intimidated to write one, only because they lack the confidence for sending information to a complete stranger. Fortunately, that stranger may soon be your next manager.

To master this tool, it is important to present your brand. The letter is a brief description of your resume, highlighting your skill sets in three paragraphs: the bait, the hook, and the catch. It is important to structure the letter to make sure every word counts.

23

Choose Keywords Carefully

The keywords you choose are a vital element to a persuasive letter that matches key skill sets the hiring manager is looking for. It also presents your qualifications and tells the hiring manager how and why you are best qualified for the position. The keywords fall into three categories, which we will go into next.

Take a moment to think of some phrases that describe your experience.

_____

_____

_____

_____

_____

_____

_____

_____

_____

_____

_____

_____

_____

_____

_____

_____

_____

24

Skill Keywords

The words chosen here should identify the skills needed to perform the position at a high level of performance. Skill words should be attributed to something that you have done during your college career that had a successful outcome. Some examples of skill keywords are: programmed, designed, created, built, wrote, planned, and trained.

List some of your skill keywords below.

_____

_____

_____

_____

_____

_____

_____

_____

_____

_____

_____

_____

_____

_____

_____

_____

_____

25

Results Keywords

It is a competitive work environment and hiring managers are looking for people that can make an immediate impact to their business. Think back in your college and work career. Did you make a positive impact to the business or group? Results-oriented words are best associated with specific numbers that impacted your performance. Some examples of results-oriented keywords are: increased, redesigned, upgraded, implemented, produced, reduced, and initiated.

List some results keywords below.

_____

_____

_____

_____

_____

_____

_____

_____

_____

_____

_____

_____

_____

_____

26

Recognition Keywords

Hiring managers like when candidates have been recognized in former jobs, organizations, and clubs. This is a good indication you will bring that business savvy to the company. Ideally, recognition phrases will include the type of individual who noted your achievement and the basis for your recognition. Some examples of recognition keywords are: honored, awarded, recognized, chosen, promoted and selected.

List your recognition keywords below.

_____

_____

_____

_____

_____

_____

_____

_____

_____

_____

_____

_____

_____

_____

_____

27

Interview Preparation

Congratulations, you did it. You sent in a great cover letter and scored the interview. But now what? Before you go in, take the time to thoroughly prepare yourself. Research the company on their official website to become an expert in their business. Google search company articles and the executives. Print all pertinent information and study before your meeting. Print out the company profile "About Us" and bring it to the interview.

Study industry trends. Find out who their customers and competitors are, and what challenges they face today. In addition, search for the latest trends on Facebook and Twitter.

Go to Glassdoor.com and read what others say about the company. This site will provide the good, bad, and ugly.

_____

_____

_____

_____

_____

_____

_____

_____

_____

_____

_____

28

LinkedIn

Search your interviewer on LinkedIn to understand his or her career path with the company and other relevant information such as education, professional association involvement, hobbies, and interests. You must have a LinkedIn profile to complete this exercise. Tip 91 will discuss how to set up a LinkedIn profile later in the book.

29

Tap Into Your Network

If you know anyone employed by the company, reach out and ask about the company's culture and what they like and dislike about their position.

Make a list of people you should contact.

_____

_____

_____

_____

_____

_____

_____

_____

_____

_____

_____

_____

_____

_____

_____

_____

_____

_____

_____

30

Practice, Practice, Practice

Be prepared to answer interview questions using the behavioral interview techniques or STAR (more about that in the following section of this book). Practice answering these anticipated questions with your family, friends, or in front of a mirror. Practice breeds perfection.

Prepare questions to ask the interviewer based on the information you have gathered researching the company.

31

What to Wear

How should you dress for the interview?

Men should wear a dark suit, solid white or blue shirt (or small pattern in those colors), and a conservative tie. Shoes shined, dark socks, matching belt, haircut, clean shaven, sideburns tight, hair neatly groomed and no cologne.

Women should wear a dark suit with a white or blue blouse (or other conservative pattern), shoes conservative (mid heel is fine—no flats), hair neatly groomed, simple earrings, minimal wrist jewelry, neck jewelry conservative, and no or very light perfume.

Make a list of your interview ensemble.

_____

_____

_____

_____

_____

_____

_____

_____

_____

_____

_____

_____

_____

32

Before the Interview Checklist

✓ Wash your car and clean the inside.

✓ Leave early to allow for traffic and plan to arrive fifteen minutes early. Check the weather the night before and plan your travel accordingly.

✓ Bring three copies of your resume on heavy stock paper.

✓ Bring a nice portfolio to take notes and use a nice pen.

✓ Bring letters of recommendation and project work that you are proud to present.

✓ Leave your phone in the car.

✓ Do not chew gum or bring in a drink.

✓ Floss your teeth before the meeting especially after lunch. Have a mint to freshen your breath.

If your first meeting is a phone screen, find a quiet space at home or in your car. Limit all potential distractions.

33

At the Interview Checklist

✓ Impress the receptionist: "Hi, I am J. Smith and I have a one o'clock meeting with Mr. White. Would you be so kind as to let him know I am here for our meeting?" Make small talk with the receptionist, weather, sports, and company news. You will be surprised to know that some receptionists have an influence with the hiring manager.

✓ When meeting the hiring manager introduce yourself and shake hands firmly with a confident tone of voice.

✓ Speak with confidence throughout the meeting and smile.

✓ Look the hiring manager in the eye throughout the meeting. Do not stare out into space. This will show you are not prepared and lack confidence.

✓ Sit up in your chair and have a good posture. Lean forward when answering questions. Do not appear to be too relaxed and overconfident.

✓ Listen to the questions and think before you answer. It is OK to pause to think of your answer. Don't be nervous—the hiring manager was in your spot when he or she was your age.

✓ Stay on track when answering the question.

✓ Be energetic and act like you belong and want the job.

34

Interview Conclusion Checklist

✓ Take notes at the appropriate time to ensure you are listening to the question.

✓ Do not discuss the compensation or benefits unless the interviewer brings them up. Sometimes the hiring manager will explain what these are, especially if the interview went well.

✓ Ask for a tour of the office or plant operations. You may get a chance to see working conditions and meet some of the colleagues. In addition, you will see company dashboards like sales performance, plant production performance, office cleanliness, and the like. This shows that you are interested in coming on board.

✓ Upon completion of the interview, thank the hiring manager for his or her time and ask what the next steps are in the process. If you sincerely feel that there is a fit and the opportunity meets your career aspirations, ask for the opportunity to start your career with the firm.

35

After the Interview Checklist

✓ Ask the hiring manager for a business card and send an e-mail the same day and a written thank you note in the US mail to arrive within two days.

✓ When you are asked to come back for a second meeting, prepare a three, six, and twelve month business development plan on how you will add value to the company. This task will build your brand and value.

✓ At this point, you will be meeting with a manager(s) from other departments and select colleagues. This is a good sign there is interest in your talent. Present your business plan to the team with confidence. Again, act like you belong.

✓ Upon completion of the meeting, this is a good time to ask about the compensation and benefits if they were not covered in the previous meeting. If they meet your expectations, stay calm.

✓ Summarize your talent to include past leadership roles, work experience, and value to the team and why you will be an asset to the company. Refer back to your business plan.

✓ Ask for the opportunity to come on board. Never ask for the job, but the opportunity to start your career.

✓ At this point, the hiring manager may make you the offer. If so, ask for the offer in writing and ask to be given time to review it with your family.

36

Behavioral Interview Techniques

Behavioral-based interview questions are based on how candidates have acted and responded in a specific situation. The logic behind this approach is that companies have pre-determined skill sets that are required for the position and that past behavior and performance predicts future behavior and job performance in the work environment. The STAR approach uses objective questions looping a situation to the outcome.

SITUATION
TASK
ACTION
RESULT

37

The STAR Approach

Situation or Task: Describe a situation that you were in or a task that you needed to accomplish. In this scenario, a specific event or situation must come to mind and not a generalized description of what you have done in the past. Remember it must be specific. Give enough information so the interviewer can paint a picture and understand. The situation can be from work, school, sport, or any relevant event.

Action: What were the specific actions you took? Keep all the focus on you and not others in the situation. You must be specific and tell exactly what you did and not what you might have done in the situation.

Result: What were the results? What was accomplished? What did you learn?

38

Brainstorm STAR Examples

Some examples you can use are group projects, work experiences, volunteer work, community services, and sports team events. Keep the situations relatively recent, during your college years. You may want to use significant events in your life such as hitting the homerun in the College World Series, election to your sorority Greek council, and special volunteer work. Remember to be specific and quantify your results. What was the specific outcome and how did it improve the situation? Include numbers and percentages. Hiring managers love to see the numbers.

_____

_____

_____

_____

_____

_____

_____

_____

_____

_____

_____

_____

_____

_____

39

Interview Buckets

These skill sets, also referred to as key core competencies, are what employers are identifying during the interview process. Not all the questions you are asked will have a positive outcome. That is fine. However, be prepared to have negative experiences ready and explain how you made the best of the situation.

40

Brainstorm Interview Buckets

The interview buckets are the key core competencies the hiring manager is going to uncover during the meeting. So, think back to the last four years and find examples that best will describe exemplary behavior.

- Some of the situations should be positive where you met goals and major accomplishments.

- The others should be situations that started out negative but either turned out positive or you made the best of the outcome.

- Your answers should come from all areas of your life and be about fairly recent situations. Going back to high school is not accepted from most companies.

In the space below, brainstorm some experiences that relate to the key core competencies listed above. Have six to eight situations thought out and ready to talk about.

_____

_____

_____

_____

_____

_____

_____

_____

_____

_____

41

How Do I Prepare For a Behavioral Interview?

Many companies using behavioral interview techniques have pre-determined skill sets required to be successful. The skill sets were covered earlier in the "Interview Buckets." Successful companies have done detailed analyses on their most successful colleagues and have determined what core competencies they all share. These competencies become the standard for future hires.

Here is a checklist of some of the things you should consider before your meeting:

✓ What are the required skill sets to be successful in this position?

✓ By joining the company, will I make the best use of my skill sets and expertise? Will the company help me to grow them further?

✓ What makes a successful candidate?

✓ What would make a candidate unsuccessful?

✓ According to your research, does the company culture fit in line with your character and career objectives?

✓ What is the company's turnover? Why do people leave the company? You will see some of this information on Glassdoor.com

✓ What do you think the most difficult part of the job will be, and do you have the skills necessary to overcome?

Keep all of these points in mind before the interview. If for any reason you feel you do not have the skill set or feel uncomfortable with half of the above considerations, you should not interview. Do yourself and the company a favor and bow out gracefully. That is OK.

42

Potential Interview Questions

You can't know ahead of time what you will be asked in an interview. But there are some common questions and areas that hiring managers often ask. Taking the time to prepare responses to some of these common questions will help avoid stress and make you appear confident and poised.

43

Sample Interview Question A

(The competency is listed in parentheses.)

Tell me about a time that you had to convince your supervisor that there was a better way to complete the work assignment? Or, tell me about a time that you had to approach your professor regarding a grade that you did not agree with? (Assertiveness)

Hint: Think of a time when you felt your way was better. We all received a grade on an exam or project where we said, "I studied really hard, this isn't right." Do not come across as confrontational. Explain the situation and how you were able to work the issue out.

_____

_____

_____

_____

_____

_____

_____

_____

_____

_____

_____

_____

_____

_____

44

Sample Interview Question B

Describe a situation when you were given a project that required a significant amount of research in an area you were not familiar with? Or, how have you prepared for an exam that required you to have researched a topic and complete a written dossier? (Research and written communication)

Hint: Think of a difficult project or test requiring much of your time and research of the topic. What were the things you did differently in your preparation?

_____

_____

_____

_____

_____

_____

_____

_____

_____

_____

_____

_____

_____

_____

45

Sample Interview Question C

Describe a situation when a teammate, classmate, or co-worker criticized you in front of others for something that you thought was not your fault? How did you respond? (Oral Communication)

Hint: Respond to the question positively. We all have made mistakes. What did you learn from this situation? Maybe it was a bad play in a game, or a customer service experience in your job where your co-worker did not agree with the way you handled the situation.

_____

_____

_____

_____

_____

_____

_____

_____

_____

_____

_____

_____

_____

_____

_____

_____

46

Sample Interview Question D

Describe a situation where you gave it your all and the desired result was not what you expected? (Ability to handle adversity)

Hint: Was it a test, group project, work situation, sporting event? Come across as positive. Share the lesson learned and what you've been able to apply that lesson learned to since then.

_____

_____

_____

_____

_____

_____

_____

_____

_____

_____

_____

_____

_____

_____

_____

_____

_____

_____

47

Sample Interview Question E

Tell me about a time that you failed to meet a deadline? How did you handle the situation? What were the things that you learned? (Time Management)

Hint: Did your professor or boss give you a project where the deadline was missed? Answer the question with sincerity and be specific on what you learned from the situation.

_____

_____

_____

_____

_____

_____

_____

_____

_____

_____

_____

_____

_____

_____

_____

_____

48

Sample Interview Question F

Describe to me how you begin to study for your finals, prepare for a large group project, or an exam? What are the things you do to be prepared? (Time Management)

Hint: What is your ritual to plan for these types of events? Do you change your day to day activities to be better prepared? More sleep, better nutrition? Do you consult with your supervisor to ensure your work hours will not affect these events?

_____

_____

_____

_____

_____

_____

_____

_____

_____

_____

_____

_____

_____

_____

_____

49

Sample Interview Question G

Describe the process you use to keep track of multiple projects? How do you ensure that you stay on task to meet the deadline? Or, tell me about a time that you had a group project and the deadline was approaching and some team members were not pulling their weight? (Commitment to Task)

Hint: Explain ways you keep organized ensuring your projects are not missed, demonstrating your commitment. Were you the person in the group that stepped up when others didn't?

_____

_____

_____

_____

_____

_____

_____

_____

_____

_____

_____

_____

_____

_____

_____

50

Sample Interview Question H

Tell me about a time that you engineered an innovative solution for a challenging task that no one else was able to handle? (Creativity and Imagination)

Hint: Did you have group projects or class assignments where your creativity put you in "Rock Star" status? Or, were you able to accomplish certain tasks in your job no one else was able to do? Did your professor or work supervisor recognize you?

_____

_____

_____

_____

_____

_____

_____

_____

_____

_____

_____

_____

_____

_____

_____

_____

51

Sample Interview Question I

Describe a situation where you had to make a decision that was not the most popular, but you felt it was the right thing to do? What was your thought process with your decision? How did others respond to your decision? Or, describe a specific situation where you needed to solve a problem with an employer or roommate? (Decision Making)

Hint: We all want to please others, but at times your values differ from others. Your answer will demonstrate your core values. These type of situations happened quite often in college, especially with roommates.

_____

_____

_____

_____

_____

_____

_____

_____

_____

_____

_____

_____

_____

_____

_____

52

Sample Interview Question J

We all have had team projects. Tell me about your last team project and your involvement with the group. Were you the team leader? Or, describe a situation that required you to rally your team to accomplish a difficult task. (Teamwork)

Hint: Think of your biggest team project recently and explain away. Were you the leader or the follower? Your answer needs to demonstrate you are a good team player.

_____

_____

_____

_____

_____

_____

_____

_____

_____

_____

_____

_____

_____

_____

_____

53

Sample Interview Question K

Describe a situation where you felt assured of how to handle it, but others had a better way to approach the problem? (Flexibility)

Hint: Think of some work examples, organization involvement or group project examples. Come across as flexible and talk about things that worked out with a positive outcome.

54

Sample Interview Question L

Describe two specific goals that you made this year and how successful were you in meeting them? What were the criteria you set that outlined your success? (Goal Setting)

Hint: Think of the goals that are relevant to your studies or organizational involvement.

_____

_____

_____

_____

_____

_____

_____

_____

_____

_____

_____

_____

_____

_____

_____

_____

_____

55

Sample Interview Question M

What is your thought process when you set your goals? (Goal Setting)

Hint: Describe goals that are SMART: be Specific, ensure they are Measurable, Achievable, Relevant to your career and the Timeframe is reasonable to achieve.

56

Sample Interview Question N

Tell me about a time when you felt extremely stressed, and how did you handle the situation? (Commitment to Task)

Hint: This has happened to everyone in college. Was it a test, roommate issue, team project, personal matters at home?

_____

_____

_____

_____

_____

_____

_____

_____

_____

_____

_____

_____

_____

_____

_____

_____

_____

57

Sample Interview Question O

Why did you choose to attend your college?

Hint: Does your university have a prominent program in your field of study? Was the school nationally recognized for research in your field of study?

60

Sample Interview Question R

Who were your favorite professors, and why?

Hint: Did you have professors who were great mentors? Did you conduct research projects with them? Were they approachable?

61

Sample Interview Question S

What is your GPA?

Hint: If your GPA is below 2.5, be prepared to explain why. Were you working to pay your way through college or did you have some distractions from home? Your character, values and work ethic may supersede the importance of the company's policy on college GPAs.

_____

_____

_____

_____

_____

_____

_____

_____

_____

_____

_____

_____

_____

_____

_____

_____

62

Sample Interview Question T

How much of your education did you finance?

Hint: Hiring managers like to know if you made a contribution to your education, demonstrating you had some "skin in the game." However, many families have monies set aside for education. It is OK to be honest and let the hiring manager know your family made contributions.

63

Sample Interview Question U

In what extra-curricular activities did you participate in college?

Hint: Were you involved in the campus community? How about clubs, professional/social organizations such as student government, your college major organization of choice, fraternity or sorority? Did you hold an office in your organization? Explain why you chose the activity.

_____

_____

_____

_____

_____

_____

_____

_____

_____

_____

_____

_____

_____

_____

_____

_____

_____

64

Sample Interview Question V

Do you have plans to continue your education?

Hint: Do you? Some companies offer reimbursement for continued education.

_____

_____

_____

_____

_____

_____

_____

_____

_____

_____

_____

_____

_____

_____

_____

_____

_____

_____

65

Sample Interview Question W

How has your education prepared you for your career?

Hint: Did you take advantage of opportunities in your career interest, such as clubs and professional organizations? If so, did you hold a leadership role? Hiring managers like to see involvement and leadership.

_____

_____

_____

_____

_____

_____

_____

_____

_____

_____

_____

_____

_____

_____

_____

_____

_____

66

Sample Interview Question X

What qualities do you feel a successful manager should have?

Hint: Think about the individuals you have worked for in the past, or your college professors. What qualities did they possess that impressed you? Did these people nurture your success to be a great student or employee?

67

Sample Interview Question Y

What type of work environment do you want to work in?

Hint: Corporate/family business, solid company culture, fast/slow paced, nurturing, competitive, open door with your supervisor, structured management trainee program, policy driven, promotional opportunities, growing business, start up/established business

68

Sample Interview Question Z

What type of manager do you want to work for?

Hint: Think of the best boss you have worked for. What qualities did he or she have? Your answer can be similar to what qualities a successful manager should have. In addition, consider the following traits in great managers: honesty, ability to communicate effectively, competent, confident, sense of humor, committed to your development, positive attitude, creative, ability to inspire those around them, intuitive of the business

69

Sample Interview Question AA

What are some of the tasks you completed for our meeting today?

Hint: Did you review the company's website, Facebook and LinkedIn postings, industry trends, competitors, company's advantages over the competitors, speak to current employees or customers? Did you review the hiring manager's LinkedIn page, checking this person's career background?

70

Sample Interview Question BB

Why are you interested in joining our company?

Hint: Industry leader, company culture matches your personality, reputation, training program, opportunities to develop skill sets and grow with the company

_____

_____

_____

_____

_____

_____

_____

_____

_____

_____

_____

_____

_____

_____

_____

_____

_____

71

Sample Interview Question CC

Are you willing to relocate?

Hint: Be honest. However, it could knock you out of consideration if you are not willing. Some companies may require you to train in a particular city. After your training, you can be re-located where needs exist within the organization.

72

Sample Interview Question DD

Are you willing to travel? If so, how much?

Hint: Traveling can be exciting for recent grads. It offers you the opportunity to see other areas of the company, customers or prospects. Look forward to traveling for the company, because it is part of your development.

_____

_____

_____

_____

_____

_____

_____

_____

_____

_____

_____

_____

_____

_____

_____

_____

_____

_____

73

Sample Interview Question EE

Is money more important to you or the opportunity to start your career?

Hint: Both are important; you want a fair salary relative to the position offered.

_____

_____

_____

_____

_____

_____

_____

_____

_____

_____

_____

_____

_____

_____

_____

_____

_____

_____

74

Sample Interview Question FF

With what range of salary will you be comfortable?

Hint: Review similar positions that are posted on job sites or salary guidelines for your career posted on Internet sites. Do not short change your talent and settle for less than the expected range of salary.

_____

_____

_____

_____

_____

_____

_____

_____

_____

_____

_____

_____

_____

_____

_____

_____

_____

_____

75

Sample Interview Question GG

How would you describe yourself to someone who has never met you?

Hint: What defines your character, strengths and qualities? What have you been told by past work supervisors or college professors? Ensure your description matches the skill sets that are needed for the position you are applying for.

_____

_____

_____

_____

_____

_____

_____

_____

_____

_____

_____

_____

_____

_____

_____

_____

_____

76

Sample Interview Question HH

Briefly describe to me every job that you had going back as far as you can remember.

Hint: This will set you apart from other candidates. Hiring managers like to see a solid work ethic before you became of legal age to work. Were you babysitting, cutting lawns, washing cars, working in the family business? Were you one of the lucky ones growing up on the family farm and up early before school to do the chores?

_____

_____

_____

_____

_____

_____

_____

_____

_____

_____

_____

_____

_____

_____

77

Sample Interview Question II

What is your most important accomplishment in the past four years?

Hint: Is it relevant to your career? Did you make a significant impact to a social/professional organization or club? Did you participate in a research project that was recognized nationally? Do not say "Graduating from college." That is expected. This can take you out of consideration for the job.

78

Sample Interview Question JJ

How would you describe your ideal career opportunity?

Hint: A career that allows me the opportunity to use my education to make an impact to the organization within a short period of time. A career that is fulfilling where I can continue to develop skill sets to be successful and a top performer.

79

Sample Interview Question KK

What goals do you currently have for your career? What are your short-term goals, two to five year goals, and your long-term goals (six to ten years)?

Hint: Your answer should be relevant to your career. How do you plan on accomplishing your goals? If this is your second interview, have your goals mapped out on a separate document. Do not say "hard work." Be more creative than the other candidate.

_____

_____

_____

_____

_____

_____

_____

_____

_____

_____

_____

_____

_____

_____

_____

_____

80

Sample Interview Question LL

How will you personally define your success and what metrics will you use?

Hint: Goals and milestones my manager sets for my success are aligned with company goals. When I am successful, my manager will be as well.

81

Sample Interview Question MM

What do you think it will take to be successful in the position for which you are interviewing?

Hint: Think about what you have done in your college career that made you successful. That is the answer to the question. In addition: coming in early, staying late, asking for assignments when others will not, communicating well with your supervisor/fellow colleagues and doing more than what is expected.

82

Sample Interview Question NN

What accomplishments have given you the most satisfaction in your life?

Hint: Think of the accomplishments that are relevant to your career. Will the accomplishments make an impact to the company? Were you a leader of a group? Did you earn regional or national status for research or class projects?

_____

_____

_____

_____

_____

_____

_____

_____

_____

_____

_____

_____

_____

_____

_____

_____

83

Sample Interview Question OO

What are some things that excite and motivate you?

Hint: This is the time to soul search. Ensure your answer is relevant to the position. For educators it could be the sight of a student finally understanding the class lesson. For those in sales professions, perhaps it's the excitement of closing the sale. For IT professions, it could be the "Aha!" moment of uncovering that software issue.

_____

_____

_____

_____

_____

_____

_____

_____

_____

_____

_____

_____

_____

_____

_____

_____

_____

_____

84

Sample Interview Question PP

What are the reasons I should hire you?

Hint: This is the moment of truth where you need to make a positive impact. Summarize your qualities to three or four competency buckets previously discussed and loop the answers to those questions in your final summary.

An example would be: "Mr./Ms. hiring manager, I am the right candidate for this position. Our conversation during our time together focused on organization, leadership, time management and assertiveness." At this point, reference your earlier answers, remembering the STAR. You have as much time as you need; however, be specific and to the point. Finally, ask for the opportunity to come on board.

85

Sample Interview Question QQ

What are your greatest strengths? Your weaknesses?

Hint: These are the toughest questions to answer. It makes many people feel extremely uncomfortable. No one likes to seem like they are bragging and we definitely do not want to share our weaknesses. Unfortunately, they need to be addressed. Regarding your strengths, you know what they are. Back up the reasons with examples.

The subject of your own weaknesses, however, takes some thinking. We all have them. Choose two areas where you could use development, and give examples. Explain what you are doing to better yourself and to overcome the weaknesses. That is the most important part of your answer.

86

Candidate Questions

At the end of the interview, you will most likely be given an opportunity to turn the tables and start asking the questions. Don't let yourself be caught off guard by the seemingly casual, "Do you have any questions for me?" This is a major chance to distinguish yourself as prepared and thoughtful. Make a list of eight to ten specific targeted questions for the interviewer. Print out this list and bring it with you to the interview.

87

Candidate Question Checklist

Here are some questions to get you started thinking about this.

- ✓ What are the most important skills and attributes needed for this position?
- ✓ What are some things about your business that keep you up at night?
- ✓ How long have you been with the organization?
- ✓ What has been your career path within the organization?
- ✓ Can you paint a picture of a typical workday?
- ✓ What is the organizational structure in your department?
- ✓ What are your organizational values? How do these values influence your decision making on a day-to-day basis?
- ✓ How would you describe your company's culture?
- ✓ What is your vision for your area of responsibility over the next two to three years?
- ✓ What challenges are you facing as a manager?
- ✓ What is your competitive advantage in the market place?
- ✓ How do you differentiate yourself from your competitors?
- ✓ Can you explain your value proposition to your prospects? Customers?
- ✓ Can you tell me about the colleagues that I would work with in your organization?
- ✓ What would exceptional performance look like in your organization the first ninety days?
- ✓ What is your management style?
- ✓ How do you typically make decisions?
- ✓ What is your preferred method of communicating with your colleagues?
- ✓ What are the key performance indicators your manager measures your success by?
- ✓ What are the key performance indicators that are measured for my success?
- ✓ How often are performance reviews conducted?
- ✓ What are the organizational goals and what metrics are used to measure the success?
- ✓ Tell me about the strategic plans of the organization? How often are they evaluated?
- ✓ How are the strategic plans communicated within the organization?

Think of some more questions that fit your particular industry or position and list them here.

88

Networking

Networking as a young professional is critical to establishing your brand. Your brand will follow you throughout your career. Therefore, it is important to do the right things now to enhance your reputation as a professional.

It is predicted the average millennial entering the work force today will have fifteen to twenty jobs before retirement. That is a significant increase from Baby Boomers and Generation X. Establishing your contacts and landing your first successful position will begin to build your reputation and credibility. It is not uncommon to find future positions through word of mouth in your network. The other alternative is searching the Internet or company job sites in which you have no established connection.

89

Networking Checklist

Here are areas to start networking in today:

✓ College professors and counselors

✓ Professional organizations

✓ High school teachers and counselors

✓ College and high school coaches

✓ Past high school and college jobs

✓ College alumni

✓ Fraternity/Sorority alumni

✓ LinkedIn groups

✓ Follow companies on LinkedIn, Facebook, and Twitter

✓ Clergy

✓ Neighbors

✓ Friends and relatives

✓ Social events such as golf outings, fundraisers, marathons

✓ Join your local chamber of commerce

✓ Internships

Who are the top priority networking contacts you should reach out to?

90

Social Media Networking

Social media networking has evolved over the last ten years. In business, it helps support and promotes the brand of companies. It is the digital footprint that defines who they are, what products and services are sold, employment talent they attract and much, much more. Social media can be an Achilles' heel to some; but to most, it is a media that has countless benefits, if implemented and managed properly.

Your brand is no different in the world of social media. If used properly, you can be the beneficiary of countless employment and business opportunities.

91

Creating Your LinkedIn Profile

For the sake of your brand and positioning yourself in business, LinkedIn is the media of choice. LinkedIn is a business-oriented social networking service that professionals use for networking, employment opportunities, company news, and much more.

_____

_____

_____

_____

_____

_____

_____

_____

_____

_____

_____

_____

_____

_____

_____

_____

_____

_____

_____

92

Photo

Use a professional headshot of just you with a solid background. Using a smart phone photo is fine. LinkedIn allows you to crop your photo to look your best. Remember to smile.

93

Headline

This is the most important field on your profile. It is the space that defines your brand and it is what future employers and others will see immediately when your LinkedIn page is opened. What defines you? Here is where you want to use action or keywords defined in your resume. Do not post your current job in your headline.

94

Summary

This is a conversation about you with the reader. It defines who you are. It is never written in third person. Write from the heart. What should you write about? Who are you? What are some things that get you excited? What are things that inspire you? What are you most proud of? What are traits and competencies you can offer? Are there certain skill sets that set you apart from others?

_____

_____

_____

_____

_____

_____

_____

_____

_____

_____

_____

_____

_____

_____

_____

_____

95

Experience

List all your relevant experience and volunteer positions in college that will create the most interest for the reader and the most opportunity for you. Word of caution, do not upload your resume because it will cause unnecessary editing. Your resume will need to be manually entered into the profile because LinkedIn will not format your resume as you see it.

96

Education

List your college and major of interest. In addition, do you have any other accreditations or certifications?

97

Interests

Again, speak from the heart. What do you truly love to do?

_____

_____

_____

_____

_____

_____

_____

_____

_____

_____

_____

_____

_____

_____

_____

_____

_____

_____

_____

_____

_____

98

Personal Stuff

Personal details: OK to leave blank unless you like to receive birthday wishes.

Advice for contacting you: cell or e-mail

Rich media: LinkedIn has the capability for you to upload videos, presentations and photos.

99

Recommendations

Another critical piece to LinkedIn. Ask your college professors and past employers for a written recommendation of your work and experiences. Future employers like to see these, especially when the content ties back into your action and keywords in your headline. Acquire a minimum of five recommendations.

_____

_____

_____

_____

_____

_____

_____

_____

_____

_____

_____

_____

_____

_____

_____

_____

_____

_____

100

Skills

Your connections can endorse your skill sets. List your skills and watch your connections endorse your talent.

101

LinkedIn Groups

Join as many as you can in your area of interest. Join your college alumni group. Groups allow you to stay connected within your field of interest and also shows future employers you are in it to win it.

Twin Design / Shutterstock.com

Appendix

Hot Careers for College Graduates

The transition from college to a career is increasingly challenging. In the current economic environment recent college graduates can benefit from essential information about employment trends and job choices. The University of California San Diego Extension has assembled the sixth annual edition of "Hot Careers for College Graduates" with a clear goal—to provide recent college graduates with a specific list of some promising career options. UC San Diego has granted permission to reprint excerpts of this study in this book to assist with your career efforts.

In this report, there are a number of positive trends for college graduates on the heels of the Great Recession of 2008. A recent survey by the National Association of Colleges and Employers found that on average businesses plan to increase the number of new college graduates they hire this year by nearly 9 percent. The objective in the "Hot Careers" report is to pinpoint where businesses are looking to expand and where job growth likely will be in the immediate future.

The UC San Diego Extension team analyzed the economic landscape, and several important trends emerged. Technology continues to drive job creation, and many of the growing careers are tied to technological changes ranging from cloud computing to the need for easily accessible data in the world of health care. The financial sector continues to need college graduates with analytical and marketing skills who can make companies more competitive. Additionally, education remains a transforming force in an economy which needs not only a skilled, but a flexible workforce.

This report uses an algorithm to identify and rank a list of "hot career" categories that can realistically be filled by recent college graduates.

Some careers on the list require additional education or training beyond a bachelor's degree, but none require a master's or doctorate degree.

Methodology: Just What Constitutes a "Hot Career"?

Wage and employment data from the United States Bureau of Labor Statistics' (BLS) Occupational Employment Statistics determine the foundational parameters of the "hot career" designation. The Hot Careers list is to be used as a broad analysis of the best jobs for people with at least a bachelor's degree.

This report used the BLS employment projections for 2012-2022 to develop a list of jobs with the most projected openings in 2022. The jobs were scored on a scale of 0-25, with the jobs that had the largest number of openings scoring 25, and those with fewer openings stepping down to lower scores. The research team also mined the BLS data to get the list of jobs with fastest expected growth. These jobs were also scored on a 25-point scale, with the fastest growing jobs getting the maximum points. Based on these two criteria, the team extracted a list of the top 40 best jobs, weighting both these criteria equally.

The forty top jobs were then evaluated for nine attributes of the work environment:

- Duration of typical work week
- Level of competition
- Frequency of conflict situations
- Indoor, environmentally controlled work space
- Time pressure
- Need to deal with unpleasant or angry people
- Responsibility for others' health and safety
- Consequences of errors
- Time spent standing

Each attribute's score was obtained from www.onetonline.org and was weighted equally on a 25-point scale.

Median pay is an essential component of a promising career, and the wages for the top 40 jobs also were obtained from the BLS and scored on a 25-point scale.

The points from the criteria of job availability and growth, work environment and wages were added for a maximum of 100 points. The list was condensed to the top 25 jobs by eliminating management and other positions that can be achieved only with several years of work experience.

The cumulative score was then used to determine the rankings of the occupations in the Hot Careers list. A fifth dimension, "bridgeability," was applied as a simple criterion to include or exclude a given career from this particular list, but did not affect the weighted total score of the career. Its sole purpose was to eliminate careers that recent college graduates could not easily "bridge to" with minimal or no training beyond an undergraduate degree. Using this methodology reveals a clear pattern as to where employment opportunities are growing.

Hot Careers Table

Code	Occupation	Cumulative Score
15-1121	Computer Systems Analysts	76.00
13-1161	Market Research Analysts and Marketing Specialists	74.57
13-2011	Accountants and Auditors	72.07
13-1111	Management Analysts	71.18
25-2021	Elementary School Teachers, Except Special Education	67.08
13-1051	Cost Estimators	67.07
13-2051	Financial Analysts	64.22

15-1141	Database Administrators	62.95
15-1131	Computer Programmers	60.28
13-1121	Meeting, Convention and Event Planners	58.33
15-1143	Computer Network Architects	57.78
29-1031	Dietitians and Nutritionists	57.25
21-1021	Child, Family, and School Social Workers	57.08
25-2012	Kindergarten Teachers, Except Special Education	56.53
21-1091	Health Educators	55.28
19-2041	Environmental Scientists and Specialists	54.75
13-1071	Human Resources Specialists	54.58
27-1024	Graphic Designers	52.97
11-9031	Education Administrators, Preschool and Childcare Center	45.83

The first column in the chart is the classification code for each job as determined by the Bureau of Labor Statistics for the Occupational Employment Statistics Database. Note: career fields contain various jobs, and the researchers looked at both jobs and careers.

Top Ten Hot Careers for 2014

1. Computer Systems Analysts

The landscape of information technology changes rapidly, and organizations throughout the globe need computer systems analysts to remain competitive and address the incredible speed of technological innovation and change.

Computer systems analysts study an organization's current computer systems and procedures and design information systems solutions to help the organization operate more efficiently and effectively. They bring business and information technology (IT) together by understanding the needs and limitations of both.

Systems analysts must understand the business field they are working in. For example, a hospital may want an analyst with a background or coursework in health management, and an analyst working for a bank may need to understand finance. Analysts work as a go-between with management and the IT department and must be able to explain complex issues in a way that both will understand. Because analysts are tasked with finding innovative solutions to computer problems, an ability to "think outside the box" is important.

The career entry pathway is also relatively broad; systems analysts may hold almost any bachelor's degree. Although a degree in computer or information science may lower barriers to entry-level hiring, it is not specifically a minimum job requirement. Understanding of computer systems, project management, and some experience writing code are just as important to secure a position in this growing field. Firms searching for individuals who can solve broad problems are increasingly hiring analysts with liberal arts or business degrees.

According to the BLS, employment of computer systems analysts is projected to grow 25 percent by 2022, much faster than the average for all occupations. Growth in cloud computing, cyber security, and mobile networks will increase demand for these workers. The BLS reported that the median annual wage for computer systems analysts was $79,680 in May 2012.

2. Market Research Analysts and Marketing Specialists

In a world where companies are constantly evaluating returns on investments, market research analysts provide essential data to help determine a company's position in the marketplace by researching their competitors and analyzing their prices, sales, and marketing methods. Using this information, they may determine potential markets, product demand, and pricing. They collect data using a variety of methods, from interviews, questionnaires, focus groups, market analysis surveys to public opinion polls and literature reviews.

Marketing specialists ensure that organizations take this information to develop the strategies and tactics to engage consumers and constituents. They focus on building effective marketing machines that include compelling websites, effective use of social media and media relations campaigns and collateral material.

The BLS reports that employment of market research analysts and specialists is projected to grow 32 percent by 2022, much faster than the average for all occupations. Employment growth will be driven by an increased use of data and market research across all industries—to understand the needs and wants of customers and to measure the effectiveness of marketing and business strategies.

According to the BLS, companies are increasingly using research on consumer behavior to develop improved marketing strategies. By doing so, companies are better able to market directly to their target population. In addition, market research provides companies and organizations with an opportunity to cut costs. According to the BLS, the median annual wage for market research analysts was $60,300 in May 2012.

3. Accountants and Auditors

"If the world wants to address our many challenges — if business wants to restore societies' trust — business must be more transparent and acknowledge that the resources we exploit or conserve and the social benefits we engender or lose, must be factored into a company's value and thus into day-to-day management," Peter Bakker, president of the World Business Council for Sustainable Development, recently argued in the Harvard Business Review. "This is not a matter of incremental change, but a radical transformation. And it's the accountants who will lead the way."

Accountants ensure that all financial transactions are accurately entered into an entity's books in a timely way, manage activities related to taxes and compliance with financial regulation, and monitor financial operations to ensure economic efficiency and transparency.

A bachelor's degree in accounting is the best way to gain an entry-level position in this field. Other degrees in closely related fields may suffice and college graduates with strong math and economics skills are viable candidates for certificate programs in accounting.

According to the BLS, the median annual wage for accountants and auditors was $63,550 in May 2012. The BLS reports that employment of accountants and auditors is projected to grow 13 percent by 2022, about as fast as the average for all occupations. In general, employment growth of accountants and auditors is expected to be closely tied to the health of the overall economy. There has been an increased focus on accounting in response to corporate scandals and recent financial crises, the BLS points out. And tighter laws and regulations, particularly in the financial sector, will likely increase the demand for accounting services as organizations seek to comply with new standards. The continued globalization of business should also lead to increased demand for accounting expertise and services related to international trade and international mergers and acquisitions.

4. Management Analysts

Optimization has become a buzzword in the world of business. Management analysts propose ways to improve an organization's efficiency--they advise managers on how to make organizations more profitable through reduced costs and increased revenues.

Management analysts determine the methods, equipment, and personnel that will be needed to complete a project or achieve an organization's goals. They propose new systems, procedures, or organizational changes, make recommendations to management through presentations or written reports, and confer with managers to ensure that the changes are working

Management analysts often specialize in certain areas, such as inventory management or reorganizing corporate structures to eliminate duplicate and nonessential jobs. Some consultants specialize in a specific industry, such as healthcare or telecommunications. In government, management analysts usually specialize by type of agency.

According to the BLS, a bachelor's degree is the typical entry-level requirement for management analysts. However, some employers prefer to hire candidates who have a master's degree in business administration (MBA); the Certified Management Consultant (CMC) designation may improve job prospects. Few colleges and universities offer formal programs in management consulting; however, many fields of study provide a suitable education because of the range of areas that management analysts address. Common fields of study include business, management, economics, political science and government, accounting, finance, marketing, psychology, computer and information science, and English.

The BLS reports that employment of management analysts is projected to grow 19 percent by 2022, faster than the average for all occupations, and the median annual wage for management analysts was $78,600 in May 2012. The BLS projects that demand for consulting services is expected to grow as organizations seek ways to improve efficiency and control costs in areas ranging from information technology to human resources.

5. Elementary School Teachers (excluding Special Education)

Education and learning experts have long argued that the success of the education system is inextricably linked to early childhood education. Elementary school teachers provide essential experiences for children as they progress through the system—they are generalists who move easily from talking about history to mathematics to geography as they influence the learning habits of their students.

Being an elementary school teacher is at once a satisfying and demanding job. Teachers are required by statute to demonstrate the ability to help students achieve prescribed scores on national, state, and district standards, even as they introduce more intangible social concepts, such as adhering to social norms, obeying classroom rules, and following rules of etiquette. Teachers spend far more time on the job than the hours spent in the classroom. After class ends, they create lesson plans, grade assignments, evaluate individual and class academic performance, devise and implement strategies to improve student progress, and communicate effectively and collaboratively with parents to ensure their charges meet specified criteria in the building blocks of future study.

All states require public elementary school teachers to have at least a bachelor's degree, as well as a teacher's license, certificate or credential; however, specific requirements vary by state. Teachers must also typically pass a background check, complete a teacher preparation program, and demonstrate classroom competence through supervised student teaching or a more lengthy and rigorous semester- or year-long teaching internship.

According to the BLS, the median annual wage for elementary school teachers was $53,400 in 2012. Employment of kindergarten and elementary school teachers is projected to grow 12 percent by 2022, about as fast as the average for all occupations. Growth is expected due to projected increases in enrollment as well as declines in student–teacher ratios; however, employment growth will vary by region.

The BLS projects that the number of students enrolling in kindergarten and elementary schools is expected to increase over the coming decade, and the number of classes needed to accommodate these students will also rise. As a result, more teachers will be required to teach these additional classes of kindergarten and elementary school students.

The BLS reports that although overall student enrollment is expected to grow, there will be some variation by region. Enrollment is expected to grow fastest in the South and West. In the Midwest, enrollment is expected to hold steady, and the Northeast is projected to have declines. As a result, employment growth for kindergarten and elementary school teachers is expected to be faster in the South and West than in the Midwest and Northeast.

6. Cost Estimators

Cost estimators combine technical expertise with the ability to collaborate with engineers, architects or other clients to achieve project goals. Accurately predicting the cost, size, and duration of future construction and manufacturing projects is vital to the survival of businesses. Cost estimators' calculations give managers or investors this information.

Cost estimators collect and analyze data in order to estimate the time, money, materials, and labor required to manufacture a product, construct a building, or provide a service. They generally specialize in a particular industry or type of product. Depending on the their area of expertise, they must have the ability to read blueprints or technical documents, use computer software to calculate estimates and analyze databases on the costs of similar projects. Some manufacturing cost estimators work in software development. Many high-technology products require a considerable amount of computer programming, and calculating the costs of software development requires significant expertise.

The typical path to entry is a bachelor's degree in a related field— construction management or building science for construction jobs, or engineering, physical sciences or mathematics for manufacturing. New hires often learn the industry by being teamed with a veteran.

The median annual wage for cost estimators was $58,860 in May 2012. According to the BLS, employment of cost estimators is projected to grow 26 percent by 2022, much faster than the average for all occupations. The BLS projects that demand for cost estimators is expected to be strong because companies need accurate cost projections to ensure that their products and services are profitable. For this reason, cost estimators are essential to companies.

Growth in the construction industry will create the majority of new jobs, the BLS reports--in particular, the construction and repair of infrastructure, including roads, bridges, airports, and subway systems, will drive demand for qualified estimators.

7. Financial Analysts

Financial analysts provide guidance to businesses and individuals making investment decisions. Financial analysts evaluate investment opportunities. They work in banks, pension funds, mutual funds, securities firms, insurance companies, and other businesses. They assess the performance of stocks, bonds, and other types of investments.

Financial analysts generally focus on trends affecting a specific industry, geographical region, or type of product. For example, an analyst may focus on a subject area such as the energy industry, a world region such as Eastern Europe, or the foreign exchange market. They must understand how new regulations, policies, and political and economic trends may affect investments.

With the globalization of business, financial analysts must not only understand how to analyze a company's investment portfolio—they must understand international trends in business and how culture and consumer growth trends affect bottom lines.

Most positions require a bachelor's degree and business schools are often the training grounds for financial analysts. A number of fields of study provide appropriate preparation, including accounting, economics, finance, statistics, mathematics, and engineering. The Financial Industry Regulatory Authority (FINRA) is the main licensing organization for the securities industry. It requires licenses for many financial analyst positions, and most of the licenses require sponsorship by an employer, so companies do not expect individuals to have these licenses before starting a job.

The median annual wage for financial analysts was $76,950 in May 2012, according to the BLS, and employment of financial analysts is projected to grow 16 percent by 2022, faster than the average for all occupations. The BLS projects that a growing range of financial products and the need for in-depth knowledge of geographic regions are expected to lead to strong employment growth.

Investment portfolios are becoming more complex, and there are more financial products available for trade. In addition, emerging markets throughout the world are providing new investment opportunities, which require expertise in geographic regions where those markets are located, the BLS reports, and restrictions on trading by banks may shift employment of financial analysts from investment banks to hedge funds and private equity groups.

8. Database Administrators

Database administrators are ubiquitous in the global economy, helping organizations store, organize and manage the exponentially increasing amounts of information in the world. They have a two-fold mission — they make sure that data are available to users and are secure from unauthorized access.

Database administrators, often called DBAs, make sure that data analysts can easily use the database to find the information they need and that the system performs as it should. DBAs sometimes work with an organization's management to understand the company's data needs and to plan the goals of the database. Database administrators are responsible for backing up systems to prevent data loss in case of a power outage or other disaster. They also ensure the integrity of the database, guaranteeing that the data stored in it come from reliable sources.

Most database administrators have a bachelor's degree in management information systems (MIS) or a computer-related field. Firms with large databases may prefer applicants who have a master's degree focusing on data or database management, typically either in computer science, information systems, or information technology. Database administrators need an understanding of database languages, the most common of which is Structured Query Language, commonly called SQL.

The Bureau of Labor Statistics projects that there will be explosive growth for DBAs in two areas — cloud computing and the healthcare industry. The increasing popularity of cloud computing services could increase the employment of DBAs at firms by 48 percent in this industry by 2022, according to the BLS, and employment growth for database administrators in healthcare industries is projected to grow by 43 percent in general medical and surgical hospitals by 2022. The median annual wage for database administrators was $77,080 in May 2012, the BLS reports, and the overall DBA employment is projected to grow 15 percent by 2022, faster than the average for all occupations.

9. Computer Programmers

The role and scope of computer programmers have changed significantly with the evolution of computing and software development in the past several decades. In the fledgling days of computing, programmers were often solitary figures writing a single program to solve an organization's problem. Today, they work collaboratively to translate designs created by developer, engineers or CEOs into programs that will advance a company's mission.

The environment for computer programmers has changed dramatically as well, with the increasing market for programs for smart phones and social media as well as the move toward open-source software. The BLS reports that with globalization and the realty that computer programming can be done from anywhere in the world, many companies are hiring programmers in countries where wages are lower. This trend is projected to limit growth for computer programmers in the United States, according to the BLS, and employment of computer programmers is projected to grow 8 percent from 2012 to 2022, about as fast as the average for all occupations.

Still, the BLS projects that many computer programmers work in computer system design and related services, an industry which is expected to grow as a result of an increasing demand for new computer software. New applications demand in the fields of mobile technology and healthcare are driving job growth in programming, and there are increasingly new opportunities for entrepreneurial programmers in the world of mobile applications, as these programmers can write and market their own software for a global market that exceeds 1 billion customers.

The BLS reports that the median annual wage for computer

programmers was $74,280 in May 2012, well above the median for most jobs in the United States.

10. Meeting, Convention, and Event Planners

Meeting and event planners can have a broad scope of responsibilities—whether it's helping a family define the details of a wedding or assisting multinational corporations with the planning of an annual event that brings together tens of thousands of employees.

The Bureau of Labor Statistics provides an overview of the types of meeting, convention and event planners:

- Association planners organize annual conferences and trade shows for professional associations.

- Corporate planners organize internal business meetings and meetings between businesses.

- Government meeting planners organize meetings for government officials and agencies.

- Convention service managers help organize major events, as employees of hotels and convention centers.

- Event planners arrange the details of a variety of events, including weddings and large parties.

- Non-profit event planners plan large events with the goal of raising donations for a charity or advocacy organization. Events may include banquets, charity races, and food drives.

Candidates with a bachelor's degree in hospitality or tourism management should have the best job opportunities. A Certified Meeting Professional (CMP) credential is also viewed favorably by potential employers. Those who have experience with virtual meeting software and social media outlets also should have an advantage.

The median annual wage for meeting, convention, and event planners was $45,810 in May 2012, according to the BLS, and employment for this career path is projected to grow 33 percent from 2012 to 2022, much faster than the average for all occupations. As businesses and organizations become increasingly international, meetings and conventions are expected to become even more important.

The Economic Landscape for Recent College Graduates

A May 2014 *U.S. News and World Report* story depicts a relatively promising outlook for 2014 college graduates.

"The 1.6 million college seniors who will be graduating in the next few weeks are getting an exciting gift – more jobs. Overall, things are looking up. The Bureau of Labor Statistics announced Friday that businesses added the most jobs in more than two years during April, and the unemployment rate dropped to the lowest it's been since 2008," according to U.S News. "Many agree this is the most promising employment outlook for new college grads in several years."

Still, the aftermath of the Great Recession of 2008 is still having a profound effect on the job market, according to a 2014 report, "The Class of 2014: The Weak Economy Is Idling Too Many Young Graduates," by the Economic Policy Institute.

"By attending and finishing college, young college graduates have made a significant down payment on their career in terms of both time and money, and they typically have very high labor force participation," according to the Economic Policy Institute report. "And because a college degree affords more opportunities in the labor market—not least of which is the fact that college graduates are often more competitive relative to non–college graduates when it comes to landing jobs not requiring a college degree—unemployment among young workers with a college degree is substantially lower than among other young workers. However, young college graduates' job prospects have deteriorated dramatically since the start of the Great Recession."

In this report, UC San Diego researchers have provided recent college graduates with some specific career paths where job growth and opportunities are promising. Our goal is to analyze the job market, with a focus on the impact of globalization, economic trends, and business growth patterns, in order to realistically predict areas where new graduates can leverage or build upon their skills to enter the workforce.

> About the Author <

John P. Doyle has over thirty years of experience as a business executive. His career has extended into small to midsize and Fortune 500 companies. John's extensive background in sales, management, production, and marketing affords him the knowledge he will share with his clients to uncover the right career opportunity.

For many years, he has been a key executive mentoring young men and woman at some of the largest businesses in the industrial services sector. John's extensive experience hiring candidates at Division I universities gives him the opportunity to coach and prepare college graduates to uncover their true potential and brand their talent to potential employers. Understanding the skill sets that are required and what it takes to start your career is what John brings to his clients.

John has worked with social media and understands the meaning of developing your personal and business brand to market yourself professionally. In addition, networking skills are extremely important in today's competitive work environment. John has networked extensively over the years and can show clients how to get noticed.